AF208218

A UNIFYING
VISION
IN ACTION

A UNIFYING
VISION
IN ACTION

AN INTRODUCTION
TO THE
BAHÁ'Í FAITH

BAHÁ'Í
PUBLISHING

EVANSTON, ILLINOIS

Bahá'í Publishing

1233 Central St., Evanston, Illinois 60201

Copyright © 2023 by the National Spiritual Assembly of the Bahá'ís of the United States

All rights reserved. Published 2023

Printed in China

26   25   24   23   4   3   2   1

ISBN 978-1-61851-238-3

Book and cover design by Patrick Falso

CONTENTS

THE BAHÁ'Í FAITH:
A BRIEF OVERVIEW

THE DAWN OF A NEW DAY

The appearance of God's Messenger is like the start of a new day, when the sun's rays release energy into the world. In this turbulent period of human history, the world is in need of a unifying vision of our true nature as human beings and of the kind of world in which we would want to live.

Bahá'ís believe that this vision is revealed in the writings of Bahá'u'lláh. Bahá'u'lláh's mission was to spiritually reawaken humanity and unite all the peoples of the world. Bahá'u'lláh's teachings form the basis of the Bahá'í Faith and offer a vision of infinite hope and healing for the world. He offers a vision of a world where the recognition of the oneness of humanity ultimately leads to lasting justice, peace, and prosperity. Bahá'u'lláh wrote,

> "My object is none other than the betterment of the world and the tranquility of its peoples."

Bahá'u'lláh taught the oneness of God and religion, the oneness of humanity and freedom from prejudice, the inherent nobility of the human being, the progressive revelation of religious truth, the development of spiritual qualities, and the integration of worship and service. The Bahá'í writings also address the fundamental equality of men and women, the harmony between religion and science, the need to eliminate extremes of wealth and poverty, the centrality of justice to all human endeavors, and the importance of education.

Around the world, people of all ages, faiths, and backgrounds are engaged in a process of community building based on the unifying teachings of Bahá'u'lláh. Through a process of prayerful study, consultation, action, and reflection, children, youth, and adults engage in their own spiritual development. They explore spiritual concepts together and apply them in their own communities.

ONE GOD

Called by different names throughout the ages, the eternal God, the Creator of the universe, is limitless, all-knowing, all-powerful, and all-loving. God is one. The reality of God is beyond human understanding, though we may find expressions of God's attributes in every created thing. Although the exact nature of God eludes us, the purpose of our lives is to recognize, love, and grow closer to Him. We may do so by striving to emulate God's attributes, such as love, compassion, generosity, justice, and mercy, in both our inner lives and our actions.

> *"The peoples of the world, of whatever race or religion, derive their inspiration from one heavenly Source, and are the subjects of one God."*
>
> - BAHÁ'U'LLÁH

ONE HUMAN FAMILY

The conviction that every individual belongs to one human family is at the heart of the Bahá'í Faith. We are all citizens and co-stewards of one planet. A growing awareness of our common heritage and interdependence allows us to strive for unity in our diversity. The Bahá'í writings assert that we share a common purpose—to carry forward an ever-advancing material and spiritual civilization. Bahá'u'lláh proclaimed the oneness of humanity and called for the removal of any cause of division that would lead people to see themselves as "us" and "them." Beyond all differences of race, culture, class, or ethnicity, regardless of differences in customs, opinions, or temperaments, every individual is a member of one gloriously diverse human family.

> *"Ye are the fruits of one tree, and the leaves of one branch. Deal ye one with another with the utmost love and harmony, with friendliness and fellowship.*
>
> – BAHÁ'U'LLÁH

ONE UNFOLDING RELIGION

Humanity's spiritual, intellectual, and moral capacities have been cultivated through the successive teachings of the Founders of the world's religions—Manifestations of God. Among Them are Krishna, Abraham, Moses, Zoroaster, Buddha, Jesus Christ, Muhammad, as well as Others Whose names may have been lost to history, and, most recently, the Báb and Bahá'u'lláh. Each religion originates with God and is suited to the age and place in which it is revealed. In essence, the religion of God is one and is progressively unfolding.

While each Manifestation has a distinct individuality and a definite mission, They all share a divinely ordained purpose—to educate all people, refine their character, and endue all created things with grace. With the coming of each Manifestation, spiritual forces are released which, over time, increasingly permeate human affairs, providing the main impulse for the further development of consciousness and society.

This process, in which the Manifestations of God have continuously provided the guidance necessary for humanity's social and spiritual evolution, is known as "progressive revelation." Bahá'u'lláh explicitly stated that after the passage of at least a thousand years, another Manifestation of God would appear.

"This is the changeless Faith of God, eternal in the past, eternal in the future."

- BAHÁ'U'LLÁH

A NEW ERA

Religion today cannot be exactly what it was in a previous era. Much of what is regarded as religion in the contemporary world must be re-examined in light of the fundamental truths Bahá'u'lláh has posited: the oneness of God, the oneness of religion, and the oneness of the human family. Bahá'u'lláh set an uncompromising standard: if religion becomes a source of separation, estrangement, or disagreement—much less violence and terror—it is best to do without it. The test of true religion is its fruits. Religion should uplift humanity, create unity, forge good character, promote the search for truth, liberate human conscience, advance social justice, and promote the betterment of the world.

All of the Founders of the world's great religions, Bahá'u'lláh explained, proclaim the same faith. He described religion as a "*radiant light and an impregnable stronghold for the protection and welfare of the peoples of the world.*" Bahá'u'lláh was also deeply concerned about the corruption and abuse of religion that had come to characterize human societies around the planet. The decline of religion, He explained, sets in when the noble and pure teachings of the world's great religions are corrupted by selfish human ideas, superstition, and the worldly quest for power. "*Should the lamp of religion be obscured,*" explained Bahá'u'lláh, "*chaos and confusion will ensue, and the lights of fairness and justice, of tranquility and peace cease to shine.*"

In a rapidly changing world, a reawakening of humanity's longing for meaning and for spiritual connection is finding expression in various forms. If religion is to exert its vital influence in this period of profound, often tumultuous change, it will need to be understood anew. Humanity will have to shed harmful conceptions and practices that masquerade as religion. The question is how to understand religion in the modern world and allow for its constructive powers to be released for the betterment of all.

"The fundamental purpose animating the Faith of God and His Religion is to safeguard the interests and promote the unity of the human race, and to foster the spirit of love and fellowship."

– BAHÁ'U'LLÁH

ORIGINS

The Bahá'í Faith was born in Persia (today Iran) in the mid-19th century. In less than 200 years it has become a universal faith present in every country in the world with adherents from virtually every national, ethnic, religious, and tribal background. The Bahá'í Faith originated with Bahá'u'lláh (1817–1892), Whose title means "the Glory of God." Bahá'ís regard Him as the latest in the succession of Divine Messengers Who founded the world's major religions. Bahá'u'lláh's coming was heralded by the Báb (1819–1850), meaning "the Gate." The Báb proclaimed His divine mission in 1844, which is considered the beginning of the Bahá'í Era—a new cycle of human history and social evolution.

Bahá'u'lláh endured a life of persecution, imprisonment, torture, and exile. While in prison, the first stirrings of a divine revelation came to Him. As Bahá'u'lláh sat with His feet in stocks and a 100-pound iron chain around His neck, the Holy Spirit of God was revealed to Him. This was an event comparable to those great moments of the ancient past when God revealed Himself to His earlier Messengers: when Moses stood before the Burning Bush; when the Buddha received enlightenment under the Bodhi tree; when the Holy Spirit, in the form of a dove, descended upon Jesus; and when the angel Gabriel appeared to Muhammad. In His writings, Bahá'u'lláh later described the experience and the essence of God's revelation coming through Him:

> *"The breezes of the All-Glorious were wafted over Me, and taught Me the knowledge of all that hath been. This thing is not from Me, but from One Who is Almighty and All-Knowing. And He bade Me lift up My voice between earth and heaven. . . ."*

Upon His release from prison, Bahá'u'lláh was banished from His homeland. As Bahá'u'lláh's spiritual teachings spread, He was further exiled. He was sentenced to imprisonment in the harshest penal colony in the Ottoman Empire, the ancient city of 'Akká, located in what is now Israel. In 1892, after a brief illness, Bahá'u'lláh passed from this life at the age of 75. His earthly remains were laid to rest in a small building next to His final residence in Bahjí. The burial sites of the Báb and Bahá'u'lláh have become sacred shrines and places of pilgrimage for Bahá'ís from around the world, who visit them to draw spiritual strength and inspiration, and to dedicate themselves to the work of creating the transformed world Bahá'u'lláh envisioned.

THE COVENANT

Whereas in the past, religious communities disagreed over the question of succession and became divided after the passing of a Messenger of God, Bahá'u'lláh put into place a system that would ensure the continuity of guidance and maintain the integrity and organic wholeness of the Bahá'í community into the future, an essential concept known to Bahá'ís as the Covenant.

In His writings, Bahá'u'lláh appointed His eldest son, 'Abdu'l-Bahá, to be the head of the Faith after His passing. 'Abdu'l-Bahá was the perfect exemplar of the Bahá'í Faith's spirit and teachings. A champion of social justice and an ambassador for international peace, He devoted His life to furthering His Father's cause and to promoting its ideals. The role 'Abdul-Bahá played as spiritual leader, authoritative interpreter, and role model is unique in all religious history. Bahá'u'lláh called His son "*the Center of My Covenant*" and identified 'Abdu'l-Bahá as His successor in His written will, thereby ensuring the unity of the Faith after His passing.

'Abdu'l-Bahá passed away peacefully in His sleep on November 28, 1921, at the age of 77. In His Will and Testament, 'Abdu'l-Bahá appointed His grandson, Shoghi Effendi Rabbani, to succeed Him as the leader, or Guardian, of the Bahá'í Faith. This appointment was an extension of the Covenant established by Bahá'u'lláh. Following the passing of the Guardian, the Universal House of Justice was established.

The Universal House of Justice, the international governing body of the Bahá'í Faith, was first elected in 1963. The Universal House of Justice is without precedent in religious

history. Nonpartisan elections, without nom-
inations or campaigns and conducted by secret
ballot, and collective decision making are
hallmarks of Bahá'í administration. These and
other principles constitute a model of just and
unified global governance.

There is no priesthood within the Bahá'í
Faith and none of the members of the elected
institutions may claim a special station.
Authority is vested in the institution and its
collective decision making. Bahá'í institutions
are not merely the means of administering
the internal aspects of Bahá'í community life.
They are also channels through which the spirit
of the Faith flows, uniting and sustaining society as humanity moves towards its collective
maturity.

WORSHIP

The writings of the Báb and Bahá'u'lláh are
considered by Bahá'ís to have been revealed by
God. As the creative Word of God, these sacred
writings have the power to touch the deepest
recesses of our hearts and transform us and the

world around us. The Bahá'í writings address the needs of the age and offer inspiration for individuals working to better themselves and their communities. Bahá'u'lláh enjoined His followers to read daily from the sacred texts:

"Immerse yourselves in the ocean of My words, that ye may unravel its secrets, and discover all the pearls of wisdom that lie hid in its depths."

Daily prayer, offered both in private and in the company of others, is regarded by Bahá'ís as essential spiritual nourishment, providing inspiration for positive personal and social change.

THE SOUL

Bahá'u'lláh affirmed that each human being possesses a distinct, rational soul that constitutes the real self. The soul has its origin in the spiritual worlds of God. It is created in the image and likeness of God, meaning that it is capable of acquiring divine qualities and heavenly attributes. The soul does not enter or leave the body and does not occupy physical space. The expressions of the soul are love and compassion, faith and courage, rational thought and imagination, and other uniquely human qualities.

When death occurs, the body returns to the world of dust, while the soul continues to progress towards God. Bahá'u'lláh wrote that the soul *"will manifest the signs of God and His attributes, and will reveal His loving kindness and bounty."* The exact nature of the afterlife remains a mystery. *"The nature of the soul after death can never be described,"* wrote Bahá'u'lláh. Heaven may be understood as a state of relative nearness to God; hell as a state of remoteness from God. One's degree of nearness to God follows as a natural consequence of his or her efforts to develop spiritually, and also depends on the grace and bounty of God. During this earthly physical existence, one can develop the spiritual qualities that will be needed in the next life, which is a spiritual existence.

"Know, verily, that the soul is a sign of God, a heavenly gem . . ."

- BAHÁ'U'LLÁH

WALKING A PATH OF SERVICE

In the Bahá'í teachings, refining one's inner character and offering service to humanity are inseparable. This twofold moral purpose helps to shape the endeavors of Bahá'ís in all areas of life. The Bahá'í teachings emphasize that each person is in charge of his or her own spiritual development. Bahá'ís have come to describe the individual journey as walking a path of service towards God. It is a path open to all of humanity—a path, Bahá'ís believe, that will allow us to build a better world together.

It is a common practice for Bahá'ís to gather with their friends and neighbors for devotionals, study circles, children's classes, the junior youth spiritual empowerment program, as well as other means for contributing to constructive social change. Bahá'ís strive to participate fully in the life of society, working shoulder to shoulder with diverse groups in a wide variety of settings to contribute to the social, material, and spiritual advancement of civilization. Whatever particular form their efforts take, Bahá'ís participate motivated by concern for the common good and with a spirit of humble service to humanity.

> *"This is worship: to serve mankind and to minister to the needs of the people. Service is prayer."*
>
> – 'ABDU'L-BAHÁ

A COLLECTIVE GLOBAL ENDEAVOR

At the heart of Bahá'í endeavors is a long-term process of community building that seeks to develop patterns of life and social structures founded on the oneness of humanity. One component of these efforts is an educational process that has developed organically in rural and urban settings around the world. Spaces are created for children, youth, and adults to explore spiritual concepts and gain capacity to apply them to their own social environments. Every soul is invited to contribute regardless of race, gender, or creed. Over time, capacities for service are being cultivated and are giving rise to individual initiatives and collective action for the betterment of society. Transformation of the individual and transformation of the community unfold simultaneously.

Beyond efforts to learn about community building at the grass roots, Bahá'ís engage in various forms of social action, through which they strive to apply spiritual principles in efforts to further material progress in diverse settings. Bahá'í institutions and agencies, as well as individuals and organizations, also participate in the prevalent discourses of their societies in diverse spaces, from academic and professional settings, to national and international forums, all with the aim of contributing to the advancement of society.

The vast changes called for in Bahá'u'lláh's teachings must occur in individuals and in the structure of society, at all levels from the family to global institutions. "*Is not the object of every Revelation,*" He proclaimed, "*to effect a transformation in the whole character of mankind, a transformation that shall manifest itself, both outwardly and inwardly, that shall affect both its inner life and external conditions?*" Bahá'ís and all who share Bahá'u'lláh's vision are working systematically to create the nucleus of a divine civilization—to build new patterns of individual and community life and new organizational structures.

"*God's purpose is none other than to usher in, in ways He alone can bring about, and the full significance of which He alone can fathom, the Great, the Golden Age of a long-divided, a long-afflicted humanity. Its present state, indeed its immediate future, is distressingly dark. Its distant future, however, is radiant, gloriously radiant—so radiant that no eye can visualize it.*"

~ SHOGHI EFFENDI

"*Ultimately, the power to transform the world is effected by love, love originating from the relationship with the divine, love ablaze among members of a community, love extended without restriction to every human being.*"

–THE UNIVERSAL HOUSE OF JUSTICE

BAHÁ'Í PRINCIPLES

THE ELIMINATION
OF PREJUDICES

The principle of the oneness of humankind is the central teaching of the Bahá'í Faith. Recognition and acceptance of this principle necessitates the abandonment of prejudice of every kind—race, class, color, gender, creed, nationality, age, material wealth—everything that people have used to consider themselves superior or inferior to others. Indeed, Bahá'u'lláh's vision for a new civilization inspires people to see themselves as citizens of one common homeland, which is the planet itself. Prejudice—false perception—blinds us to the fact that every person is essentially a spiritual being with unique talents and capacities, a *"mine rich in gems of inestimable value."*

"So powerful is the light of unity that it can illuminate the whole earth."

- BAHÁ'U'LLÁH

> *"The diversity in the human family should be the cause of love and harmony, as it is in music where many different notes blend together in the making of a perfect chord."*
>
> – 'ABDU'L-BAHÁ

JUSTICE AND UNITY

Justice is necessary to bring about unity in diversity. Unifying approaches are necessary to bring about justice. In an era of rapid, often unsettling change, when society feels increasingly polarized, Bahá'ís look for sensible, empowering, and unifying solutions. Justice requires universal participation. Social change can't be an effort by one segment of humanity to impose its vision on another, however altruistic the motivation may be. We must leave behind a concept of power as a means of domination or superiority, based on contest, contention, division, or cultural difference. The Bahá'í framework is intended to release, encourage, and channel a different kind of power: the power of the human spirit, the power of unity, of love, of humble service, of pure deeds.

Humanity is engaged in a long process of social evolution and currently stands on the brink of the next stage of its development. Two inseparable processes, one of disintegration and the other of integration, are propelling humanity forward. The process of disintegration is visible in the violence, war, and corruption that go together with the collapse of an outmoded order now incapable of dealing with the needs of a maturing world. The tensions, divisions, and injustices that currently beset the world are symptoms of a longstanding illness—a spiritual disorder that shows up in rampant materialism, widespread moral decay, and a deeply ingrained racial prejudice. No one is immune to this disorder—we are all members of society and to some degree suffer the effects of its maladies. From a Bahá'í perspective, though, there is a promise of healing.

Accepting our oneness challenges many current assumptions. When relationships among community members and their institutions are characterized by love and justice, all have the opportunity to use their God-given attributes to advance social good. Bahá'ís and those who share this vision are working to advance this process of transformation. The Bahá'í community recognizes the many challenges it faces as it strives to live up to its own lofty ideals. It is work that will take generations. This monumental task is approached with a humble attitude of learning, starting with small efforts in our own neighborhoods. The main thrust of Bahá'í efforts toward social change is to build vibrant communities characterized by unity in diversity, mutual support, and collective well-being.

> *"The best beloved of all things in My sight is Justice."*
>
> – BAHÁ'U'LLÁH

"Cleave unto that which draweth you together and uniteth you."

– BAHÁ'U'LLÁH

PEACE

The Bahá'í writings are replete with references to universal peace—"*the supreme goal of all mankind.*" One of the most entrenched obstacles to peace is the widespread and uncritical acceptance of the proposition that human beings are incorrigibly selfish and aggressive. The vision of Bahá'u'lláh challenges the assumption that self-interest drives prosperity and that progress depends on its expression through relentless competition. Deeper awareness of our spiritual nature will inspire new approaches and systems which, because they are consistent with the inherent nobility of humanity, will foster harmony and cooperation instead of competition and conflict.

> *"When a thought of war comes, oppose it by a stronger thought of peace. A thought of hatred must be destroyed by a more powerful thought of love."*
>
> – 'ABDU'L-BAHÁ

EQUALITY OF MEN AND WOMEN

Another prerequisite for building a united world is the achievement of full equality between women and men. There are no grounds, moral, practical, or biological, upon which denial of the equality of men and women can be justified. Gender prejudice perpetrates injustice against women and promotes harmful attitudes and habits in men that are carried from the family to the workplace, to economic and political life, and ultimately to relations among countries. The establishment of the equality between women and men will be essential in ushering in an era of peace and prosperity.

> *"The world of humanity has two wings—one is women and the other men. Not until both wings are equally developed can the bird fly. Should one wing remain weak, flight is impossible."*
>
> - 'ABDU'L-BAHÁ

ELIMINATION OF THE EXTREMES OF WEALTH AND POVERTY

For the material and spiritual dimensions of civilization to advance in harmony, prosperity cannot be understood as the mere accumulation of personal wealth. The current extremes of wealth and poverty in the world are becoming ever more untenable. There is an inherent moral dimension to the generation, distribution, and utilization of wealth and resources, which needs to be reflected in more equitable economic structures and voluntary individual behavior. As new patterns emerge, material resources will increasingly be used to facilitate access to knowledge for all people and to uplift and edify the life of the whole of society.

One of the key aims of the Bahá'í Faith is the elimination of the extremes of wealth and poverty on a global scale. The Universal House of Justice stated, "*The welfare of any segment of humanity is inextricably bound up with the welfare of the whole. Humanity's collective life suffers when any one group thinks of its own well-being in isolation from that of its neighbours.*" Wealth should exist to serve humanity and its use should be in accord with spiritual principles. New systems must be created in this light. Achieving such a vision requires individual and collective transformation, based on learning over time and through experience how to put spiritual principles into practice.

HARMONY OF SCIENCE AND RELIGION

True religion is in harmony with science. When understood as complementary, science and religion provide people with powerful means to gain new and wondrous insights into reality and to shape the world around them, and each system benefits from an appropriate degree of influence from the other. Science, when devoid of the perspective of religion, can become vulnerable to dogmatic materialism. Religion, when devoid of science, falls prey to superstition and blind imitation of the past. The Bahá'í teachings state:

"Put all your beliefs into harmony with science; there can be no opposition, for truth is one. When religion, shorn of its superstitions, traditions, and unintelligent dogmas, shows its conformity with science, then will there be a great unifying, cleansing force in the world which will sweep before it all wars, disagreements, discords and struggles—and then will mankind be united in the power of the Love of God."

– 'ABDU'L-BAHÁ

UNIVERSAL EDUCATION

The Bahá'í writings promote universal education for all. Education is of vital importance and must address both intellectual and spiritual development. Bahá'ís see the young as the most precious treasure a community can possess, and education should help young people achieve their highest potential. The Bahá'í writings especially emphasize the importance of educating women and girls, both for their own advancement and because it is through educated mothers that the benefits of knowledge can be most effectively and rapidly diffused throughout society. Ultimately, the aim is for children to increasingly grow up free from all forms of prejudice, recognizing the oneness of humanity and appreciating the innate dignity and nobility of every human being. It is through education that we can all contribute to an ever-advancing civilization.

> *"The primary, the most urgent requirement is the promotion of education. It is inconceivable that any nation should achieve prosperity and success unless this paramount, this fundamental concern is carried forward."*
>
> – 'ABDU'L-BAHÁ

A HARMONIOUS RELATIONSHIP WITH NATURE

The wealth and wonders of the earth are the common heritage of all people, who deserve just and equitable access to its resources. It is undeniable that the current world order has failed to protect the environment from ruinous damage. Society attaches absolute value to expansion, acquisition, and the constant creation and gratification of wants. Clearly, such goals are not sustainable. As more and more people have come to recognize humanity's interconnection with and dependence on the environment, however, they have accepted that our unique impact carries with it the inescapable duty to nurture and protect the natural world.

If humanity's relationship with the natural world is to be refashioned, notions of progress, civilization, and development will need to be redefined. A global civilization in a sustainable relationship with the natural world has never existed. It therefore calls for a process of learning on a global scale. A flourishing global civilization in harmony with the natural environment is a vision toward which growing numbers are laboring. The world that beckons is one of integration and balance, beauty, and maturity.

> *"This span of earth is but one homeland and one habitation."*
>
> – BAHÁ'U'LLÁH

A SELECTION OF
BAHÁ'Í PRAYERS

I have risen this morning by Thy grace, O my God, and left my home trusting wholly in Thee, and committing myself to Thy care. Send down, then, upon me, out of the heaven of Thy mercy, a blessing from Thy side, and enable me to return home in safety even as Thou didst enable me to set out under Thy protection with my thoughts fixed steadfastly upon Thee.

There is none other God but Thee, the One, the Incomparable, the All-Knowing, the All-Wise.

—BAHÁ'U'LLÁH

Thy name is my healing, O my God, and remembrance of Thee is my remedy. Nearness to Thee is my hope, and love for Thee is my companion. Thy mercy to me is my healing and my succor in both this world and the world to come. Thou, verily, art the All-Bountiful, the All-Knowing, the All-Wise.

—BAHÁ'U'LLÁH

Blessed is the spot, and the house, and the place, and the city, and the heart, and the mountain, and the refuge, and the cave, and the valley, and the land, and the sea, and the island, and the meadow where mention of God hath been made, and His praise glorified.

—BAHÁ'U'LLÁH

Create in me a pure heart, O my God, and renew a tranquil conscience within me, O my Hope! Through the spirit of power confirm Thou me in Thy Cause, O my Best-Beloved, and by the light of Thy glory reveal unto me Thy path, O Thou the Goal of my desire! Through the power of Thy transcendent might lift me up unto the heaven of Thy holiness, O Source of my being, and by the breezes of Thine eternity gladden me, O Thou Who art my God! Let Thine everlasting melodies breathe tranquility on me, O my Companion, and let the riches of Thine ancient countenance deliver me from all except Thee, O my Master, and let the tidings of the revelation of Thine incorruptible Essence bring me joy, O Thou

Who art the most manifest of the manifest and
the most hidden of the hidden!

—BAHÁ'U'LLÁH

O God, guide me, protect me, make of me a
shining lamp and a brilliant star. Thou art the
Mighty and the Powerful.

—'ABDU'L-BAHÁ

TO LEARN MORE VISIT
Bahai.org
Bahai.us
Bic.org
Bahaibookstore.com
Or call 1-800-22-UNITE

NOTES

The Bahá'í Faith: A Brief Overview

THE DAWN OF A NEW DAY
The text in this section comes from *The Bahá'ís*, pp. 18, 24, 35, 50. The quotation from Bahá'u'lláh can be found in *Gleanings from the Writings of Bahá'u'lláh*, no. 131.2.

ONE GOD
The text in this section comes from *The Bahá'ís*, pp. 10, 36. The quotation from Bahá'u'lláh can be found in *Gleanings from Writings of Bahá'u'lláh*, no. 111.1.

ONE HUMAN FAMILY
The text in this section comes from *The Bahá'ís*, pp. 13, 10. The quotation from Bahá'u'lláh can be found in *Gleanings from the Writings of Bahá'u'lláh*, no. 132.3.

ONE UNFOLDING RELIGION

The text in this section comes from *The Bahá'ís,* pp. 10, 39. The quotation from Bahá'u'lláh can be found in *Gleanings from the Writings of Bahá'u'lláh,* no. 70.2.

A NEW ERA

The text in this section comes from *The Bahá'ís,* pp. 6, 8. The quotation from Bahá'u'lláh can be found in *Gleanings from the Writings of Bahá'u'lláh,* no. 110.1.

ORIGINS

The text in this section comes from *The Bahá'ís,* pp. 11, 25, 26–27. The quotation from Bahá'u'lláh can be found in "Súriy-i-Haykal," *The Summons of the Lord of Hosts,* ¶192.

THE COVENANT

The text in this section comes from *The Bahá'ís,* pp. 11, 73, 74, 77, 80, 81.

WORSHIP

The text in this section comes from *The Bahá'ís,* p. 11. The quotation from Bahá'u'lláh can be found in *Gleanings from the Writings of Bahá'u'lláh,* no. 70.2.

THE SOUL
The text in this section comes from *The Bahá'ís*, pp. 42–43. The quotation from Bahá'u'lláh can be found in *Gleanings from the Writings of Bahá'u'lláh*, no. 82.1.

WALKING A PATH OF SERVICE
The text in this section comes from *The Bahá'ís*, pp. 46, 48, 62. The quotation from 'Abdu'l-Bahá can be found in *Paris Talks*, no. 55.1.

A COLLECTIVE GLOBAL ENDEAVOR
The text in this section comes from *A Spiritual Path to Unity and Social Justice*, p. 9; *The Bahá'ís*, pp. 8, 9, 94. The quotation from Shoghi Effendi can be found in *The Promised Day Is Come*, ¶286. The quotation from the Universal House of Justice can be found in a letter dated 22 July 2020 to the Bahá'ís of the United States, https://www.bahai.org/library/authoritative-texts/the-universal-house-of-justice/messages/20200722_001/20200722_001.pdf.

Bahá'í Principles

THE ELIMINATION OF PREJUDICES
The text in this section comes from *The Bahá'ís*, p. 14. The quotation from Bahá'u'lláh can be found in *Gleanings from the Writings of Bahá'u'lláh*, no. 133.3. The quotation from 'Abdu'l-Bahá can be found in *Paris Talks*, no. 15.7.

JUSTICE AND UNITY
The text in this section comes from *A Spiritual Path to Unity and Social Justice*, pp. 4, 6, 7, 9, 12, 15. The quotations from Bahá'u'lláh can be found in The Hidden Words, Arabic no. 2; *Gleanings from the Writings of Bahá'u'lláh*, no. 111.1.

PEACE
The text in this section comes from *The Bahá'ís*, p. 92. The quotation from 'Abdu'l-Bahá can be found in *Paris Talks*, no. 6.7.

EQUALITY OF MEN AND WOMEN
The text in this section comes from *The Bahá'ís*, p. 37. The quotation from 'Abdu'l-Bahá can be found in *Selections from the Writings of 'Abdu'l-Bahá*, no. 227.18.

ELIMINATION OF THE EXTREMES OF WEALTH AND POVERTY

The text in this section comes from *The Bahá'ís,* p. 93. The quotation from the Universal House of Justice can be found in a letter dated 1 March 2017 to the Bahá'ís of the World, https://universalhouseofjustice.bahai.org/involvement-life-society/20170301_001.

HARMONY OF SCIENCE AND RELIGION

The text in this section comes from *The Bahá'ís,* p. 8. The quotation from 'Abdu'l-Bahá can be found in *Paris Talks,* no. 44.26.

UNIVERSAL EDUCATION

The text in this section comes from *The Bahá'ís,* pp. 56–57 and "Children's Classes," https://www.bahai.org/action/family-life-children/childrens-classes. The quotation from 'Abdu'l-Bahá can be found in *The Secret of Divine Civilization,* ¶193.

A HARMONIOUS RELATIONSHIP WITH NATURE

The text in this section comes from *One Habitation,* pp. 2, 9, 20; *The Bahá'ís,* p. 94. The quotation from Bahá'u'lláh can be found in *Tablets of Bahá'u'lláh,* no. 6.26.

A Selection of Bahá'í Prayers

The prayers included here can be found in *Bahá'í Prayers,* pp. 122, 94, i, 164, 29.

BIBLIOGRAPHY

Works of Bahá'u'lláh

Gleanings from the Writings of Bahá'u'lláh. Translated by Shoghi Effendi. Wilmette, IL: Bahá'í Publishing, 2005.

The Hidden Words. Translated by Shoghi Effendi. Wilmette, IL: Bahá'í Publishing, 2002.

The Summons of the Lord of Hosts. Wilmette, IL: Bahá'í Publishing, 2006.

Tablets of Bahá'u'lláh revealed after the Kitáb-i-Aqdas. Compiled by the Research Department of the Universal House of Justice. Translated by Habib Taherzadeh et al. Wilmette, IL: Bahá'í Publishing Trust, 1988.

Works of 'Abdu'l-Bahá

Paris Talks: Addresses Given By 'Abdu'l-Bahá in Paris in 1911. Wilmette, IL: Bahá'í Publishing, 2011.

The Secret of Divine Civilization. Translated by Marzieh Gail and Ali-Kuli Khan. Wilmette, IL: Bahá'í Publishing, 2007.

Selections from the Writings of 'Abdu'l-Bahá. Compiled by the Research Department of the Universal House of Justice. Translated by a Committee at the Bahá'í World Center and Marzieh Gail. Wilmette, IL: Bahá'í Publishing, 2010.

Works of Shoghi Effendi

The Promised Day Is Come. Wilmette, IL: Bahá'í Publishing Trust, 1996.

Bahá'í Compilations

Bahá'í Prayers: A Selection of Prayers Revealed by Bahá'u'lláh, the Báb, and 'Abdu'l-Bahá. New ed. Wilmette, IL: Bahá'í Publishing Trust, 2002.

Other Sources

The Bahá'ís. Bahá'í International Community, 2017.

One Planet, One Habitation: A Bahá'í Perspective on Recasting Humanity's Relationship with the Natural World. Bahá'í International Community, 2022.

A Spiritual Path to Unity and Social Justice: The Bahá'í Faith in America. National Spiritual Assembly of the Bahá'ís of the United States, 2021.